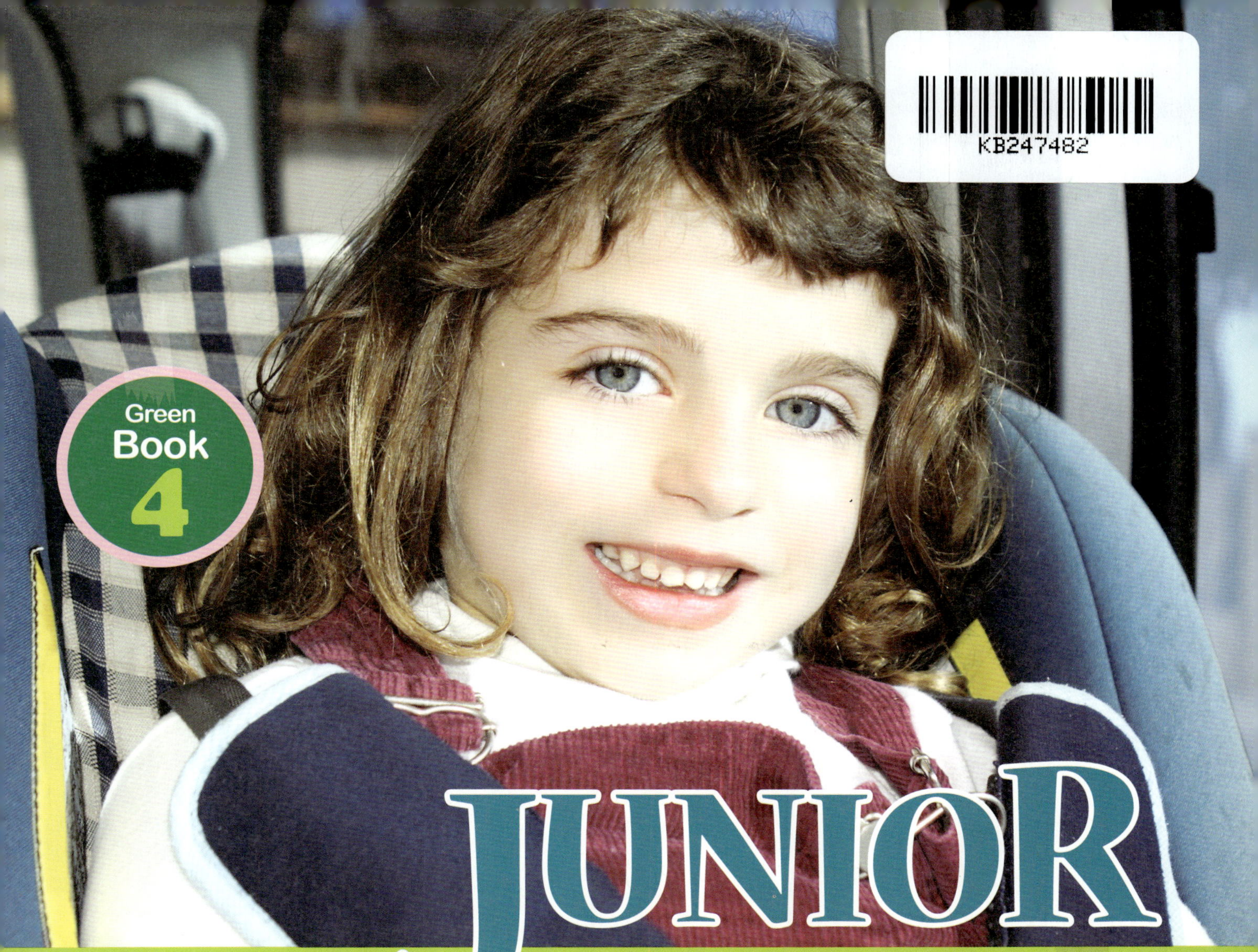

Green Book 4

JUNIOR READING Start

iambooks

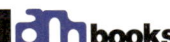

THE JUNIOR READING Start
Green Book 4

© 2011 I am Books

Published by
I am Books
327—32   1116ho, Daeroung Techno Town 12cha
Gasan—dong, Kumcheon—gu, Seoul, Korea 153—802
TEL 82—2—6343—0999
FAX 82—2—6343—0995~6
www.iambooks.co.kr

Publisher	Sangwook Oh, Sunghyun Shin
Author	TIMES CORE The Junior Times
Editor	Sungwon Lee, Dahhyun Gang, Jinhee Lee
Design	Mijung Oh, Ran Park
Illustrations	Soyoung Cho
Marketing	Shindong Jang, Shinkuk Jo, Misun Jang

ISBN 978—89—6398—070—6 64740

Green
Book
4

JUNIOR
READING Start

How to **Study** This Book

01 Before reading articles, listen to audio files carefully two or three times.

02 Underline words that you are not familiar with, reading aloud the article.

03 Read the article one more time, making a guess the meaning of words.

04 Look up the dictionary to find out the meaning of words.

05 Memorize words that you don't know and try to solve the word tip quiz.

06 Read the article once again and answer the questions.

07 Lastly, listen to the audio file one more time focusing on the words you've learned.

CONTENTS

What to Do When Earthquakes Happen

Japan was hit by a very strong earthquake on March 11. Many houses and buildings were destroyed. Many people lost their family members and friends, too. Earthquakes are very dangerous. Korea can be hit by earthquakes, too. So, you need to know what to do when they happen.

When an earthquake happens, try to stay cool. But act quickly. Get away from anything that can fall on you. Also, stay away from glass and other breakable items. Then, crawl under a piece of strong furniture. Do not hide under a chair or a small desk. If you are outside, stay away from trees and buildings. Look for an open area. Try to remember these tips. They are very important to remember!

Staff reporter Liz Ahn

Comprehension

Complete the sentences by filling in the blanks.

(a) Japan was _____ by a very _____ earthquake on March 11.

(b) You should stay away from _____ and other _____ items.

(c) If you are outside, _____ _____ _____ trees and buildings.

(d) You need to _____ what to do when an earthquake _____.

(e) _____ under a piece of _____ furniture.

Word Tip

▮ be hit by	▮ be destroyed	▮ lost	▮ family member
_____	_____	_____	_____
▮ dangerous	▮ need to	▮ happen	▮ try to
_____	_____	_____	_____
▮ stay cool	▮ 빨리 행동하다	▮ ~에서 도망치다	▮ ~위로 떨어지다
_____	_____	_____	_____
▮ 깨질 수 있는	▮ 물건	▮ 가구	▮ ~을 찾다
_____	_____	_____	_____

 **Question** **Vocabulary I**

Let's learn how to spell the important words in the article!

(a) **E** __ __ __ __ __ __ __ __ __ __

(b) **D** __ __ __ __ __ __

(c) **F** __ __ __

(d) **R** __ __ __ __ __ __ __

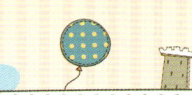

Find the words below that describe what to do when an earthquake happens.

Cool / Slow / Cushion / Quick / Furniture
Window / Crawl / Hide / Jump / Door

(a) **C** __ __ __

(b) **Q** __ __ __ __

(c) **F** __ __ __ __ __ __ __ __

(d) **C** __ __ __ __

(e) **H** __ __ __

Your Heart Is Very Important!

Close your eyes for a moment. Put your right hand on the left side of your chest. What can you feel? Can you feel your heartbeat? Your heart is beating all the time. It is a very important organ. But how much do you know about it?

Your heart is not very big, but it is very important. In fact, you cannot live without it! It pumps blood throughout your body. It weighs about 300 grams. Women's hearts beat faster than men's. Your heart beats about 70 times per minute. It beats 100,000 times a day and about 35 million times a year! So, can you guess how many times it will beat during your lifetime? Why don't you count it with your friends?

Staff reporter Liz Ahn

Read the questions and answer the following.

(a) Look at the words below.

> Heart   Hand   Chest

What is talked about in the article?

H __ __ __ __

(b) Think of the words that start with the letter 'h'!

Hint: Heart

① _____

② _____

③ _____

④ _____

(c) Why is your heart very important?

_____

_____

Word Tip

▌ close one's eyes
_____

▌ for a moment
_____

▌ chest
_____

▌ heartbeat
_____

▌ beat
_____

▌ all the time
_____

▌ in fact
_____

▌ 피, 혈액
_____

▌ 도처에, 온 사방에
_____

▌ 더 빨리
_____

▌ 추측하다
_____

▌ ~동안
_____

▌ 일생
_____

▌ 세다
_____

 Writing

Let's make sentences by filling in the blanks.

organ / count / beating / chest

(a) Put your right hand on the left side of your **c** __ __ __ __ .

(b) Your heart is **b** __ __ __ __ __ __ all the time. It is a very important **o** __ __ __ __ .

(c) Why don't you **c** __ __ __ __ your heartbeat with your friends?

 Comprehension

Read the text one more time. Explain about the heart to your friends.

_____

_____

04 Question Structure

Match up the pictures and words to make the right sentences.

Your heart   ⓐ   ① blood throughout your body.

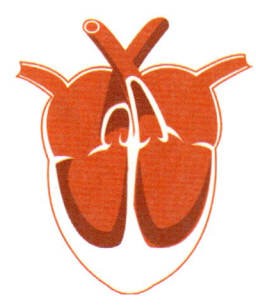

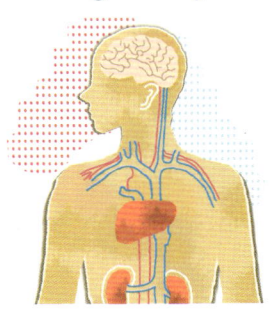

It pumps   ⓑ   ② 100,000 times a day and about 35 million times a year!

It beats   ⓒ   ③ is beating all the time.

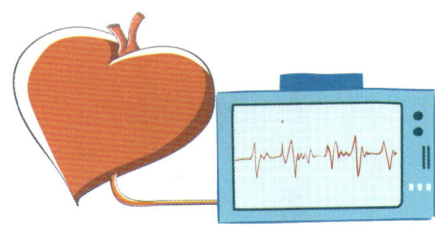

The Colors of Spring

Look around! Spring is here! Spring is the most colorful season of the year. In winter, the world was gray and white. We couldn't see many flowers and green trees in the cold season. But as the weather gets warmer, colorful flowers are blooming!

What colors can you see in spring? In fact, you can see so many different colors in this warm season. First, you can see cute yellow flowers. You can also see yellow butterflies. Soon, many other beautiful flowers will bloom. The world will be filled with pink, white, red, purple, and orange flowers! We can also see the color green! The trees will begin to bud, too. Aren't you excited to see all the different colors in spring? Let's enjoy this colorful season!

Staff reporter Liz Ahn

 **Question** **Vocabulary**

Read the questions and answer the following.

(a) Look at the words below.

Color   Spring   Flower

What is talked about in the article?

S __ __ __ __ __

(b) Think of the words that start with the letter 'S'!

Hint: Spring

① _____

② _____

③ _____

④ _____

(c) What colors can you see in spring?

_____

_____

Word Tip

▮ look around
_____
▮ colorful
_____
▮ season
_____
▮ gray
_____
▮ weather
_____
▮ bloom
_____
▮ cute
_____
▮ butterfly
_____
▮ be filled with
_____
▮ purple
_____
▮ bud
_____
▮ excited
_____
▮ enjoy
_____
▮ 귀여운
_____
▮ 꽃
_____
▮ 따뜻한
_____
▮ 봄
_____
▮ 다른
_____
▮ 겨울
_____
▮ 사실은, 실제로
_____

Writing

Let's make sentences by filling in the blanks.

blooming / filled with / colorful / warmer

(a) Spring is the most **c** __ __ __ __ __ __ __ season of the year.

(b) As the weather gets **w** __ __ __ __ __, colorful flowers are
   b __ __ __ __ __ __ __ !

(c) The world will be **f** __ __ __ __ __ **w** __ __ __ pink, white, red, purple,
and orange flowers!

Comprehension

Look at the picture. Try to explain the picture.

_____

_____

 **Question** **Structure**

Match up the pictures and words to make the right sentences.

You can see   ⓐ   ① begin to bud.

The world will   ⓑ   ② so many different colors in this warm season.

The trees will   ⓒ   ③ be filled with pink, white, red, purple, and orange flowers!

Watch Out for Yellow Dust!

Spring is a beautiful season. However, there is one bad thing about spring - yellow dust. Yellow dust blows over Korea from China and Mongolia every year. It can be bad for your health. It contains harmful materials.

Yellow dust can cause many health problems. It can hurt your eyes, nose, and throat. Sometimes it can also make you feel dizzy. This is because yellow dust contains bad things. This year's yellow dust is especially harmful. When yellow dust blows, try to stay inside. Keep your windows and doors closed. If you have to go out, wear your mask. Washing your hands often is also important. Drinking a lot of water and eating strawberries and pork are helpful, too.

Staff reporter Liz Ahn

Read the questions and answer the following.

(a) Look at the words below.

> Mask   Pork   Yellow   Dust

What is talked about in the article?

Y __ __ __ __ __   **D** __ __ __

(b) Think of the words that start with the letter 'Y'!

Hint: Yellow Dust

① _____

② _____

③ _____

④ _____

(c) What health problems can be caused by yellow dust?

_____

_____

Word Tip	
▌season	
▌yellow dust	
▌blow	
▌contain	
▌harmful	
▌material	
▌cause	
▌hurt	
▌throat	
▌sometimes	
▌dizzy	
▌especially	
▌~하려고 노력하다	
▌안에 머무르다	
▌~해야 한다	
▌마스크를 쓰다	
▌손을 씻다	
▌돼지고기	
▌도움이 되는	

Let's make sentences by filling in the blanks.

> inside / harmful / blows over / closed

(a) Yellow dust **b** __ __ __ __ **o** __ __ __ Korea from China and Mongolia every year.

(b) It contains **h** __ __ __ __ __ __ materials.

(c) When yellow dust blows, try to stay **i** __ __ __ __ __. Keep your windows and doors **c** __ __ __ __ __.

03 **Question** Comprehension

Look at the picture. Try to explain the picture.

_____

_____

04 Question Structure

Match up the pictures and words to make the right sentences.

Drinking ⓐ

① a lot of water and eating strawberries and pork are helpful.

Spring ⓑ

② your hands often is also important.

Washing ⓒ

③ is a beautiful season.

The Earth Is Amazing!

The Earth is our home. It is also home to many other animals and plants. The Earth is a beautiful planet. It is an amazing place, too. Let's learn some interesting facts about the Earth!

The Earth is about 4.5 billion years old. It is always moving. It spins while traveling around the Sun in a big circle. The Earth is the third closest planet to the Sun. The highest point on the Earth is the top of Mt. Everest. The Earth is also called the "Blue Planet". It looks blue from outer space because 70 percent of the Earth's surface is covered with oceans. The Pacific Ocean is the largest ocean. Why don't you find out some more interesting facts about the Earth?

Staff reporter Liz Ahn

Read the questions and answer the following.

(a) Look at the words below.

> Oceans   Earth   Sun

What is talked about in the article?

E __ __ __ __

(b) Think of the words that start with the letter 'E'!

Hint: Earth

① _____

② _____

③ _____

④ _____

(c) How old is the Earth?

_____

Word Tip
▮ Earth
▮ animal
▮ plant
▮ planet
▮ amazing
▮ place
▮ learn
▮ interesting
▮ fact
▮ billion
▮ spin
▮ travel around
▮ circle
▮ third
▮ the closest (close의 최상급)
▮ the highest (high의 최상급)
▮ point
▮ 정상, 꼭대기
▮ ~라고 불리다
▮ 우주 공간
▮ 표면
▮ ~로 덮여있다
▮ 대양
▮ 태평양
▮ 가장 큰
▮ ~하는 것이 어때?
▮ 발견하다, 찾다

Writing

Let's make sentences by filling in the blanks.

animals / traveling / around / planet

(a) The Earth is home to many other **a** __ __ __ __ __ __ and plants.

(b) It spins while **t** __ __ __ __ __ __ __ __ **a** __ __ __ __ __ the Sun in a big circle.

(c) The Earth is also called the "Blue **P** __ __ __ __ __".

Comprehension

Look at the picture. Try to explain the picture.

_____

_____

 **Question** **Structure**

Match up the pictures and words to make the right sentences.

It is also home to   ⓐ

① on the Earth is the top of Mt. Everest.

The highest point   ⓑ

② is the largest ocean.

The Pacific Ocean   ⓒ

③ many other animals and plants.

Say Hello to Your Neighbors!

Do you know who lives next door? Sadly, many children don't know their neighbors' faces. I know you are busy with many things. Maybe you don't have much time to spend with your neighbors. But making friends with them is not difficult. Just say hello to them first!

I'm sure there are many houses in your town. It is hard to know everyone in your neighborhood. But having some good neighbors is a good thing. They can be your best friends. They can also help you when you need someone's help. If you want to make friends with your neighbors, say hello to them first. Of course don't forget to smile brightly. Remember that having good neighbors can make your life happier!

Staff reporter Liz Ahn

Comprehension

Complete the sentences by filling in the blanks.

(a) Sadly, many children don't _____ their neighbors' _____.

(b) Making _____ with your neighbors is not _____.

(c) They can _____ you when you need someone's _____.

(d) Don't _____ to smile _____ when saying hello to your neighbors.

(e) _____ that having good neighbors can make your life _____!

Word Tip

▮ next door	▮ sadly	▮ neighbor	▮ face
▮ be busy with	▮ maybe	▮ spend	▮ make friends with
▮ 마을, 동네	▮ 물론	▮ ~을 잊다	▮ 밝게
▮ 기억하다	▮ 더 행복한		

 Question **Vocabulary** I

Let's learn how to spell the important words from the article!

(a) **D** __ __ __

(b) **B** __ __ __

(c) **S** __ __ __ __

(d) **H** __ __ __ __

 **Question** **Vocabulary II**

Find the words below that describe how to make friends with your neighbors.

> Good / Awful / Energy / First / Help
> Last / Smile / Friend / Watch / Forgive

(a) **G** __ __ __

(b) **F** __ __ __ __

(c) **H** __ __ __

(d) **S** __ __ __ __

(e) **F** __ __ __ __ __

Flowers Make Our Lives More Special!

All kinds of flowers bloom in spring. Soon, the world will be covered with colorful flowers. Seeing beautiful flowers makes us happy. Flowers also make our lives more special!

Everyone loves beautiful flowers. In fact, flowers are an important part of our lives. We give beautiful flowers to our loved ones on special days. For example, flowers are used for birthday parties, wedding ceremonies, entrance ceremonies, and graduation ceremonies. We also give our parents carnations on Parents' Day to express our love. Giving flowers to someone is like saying "I love you." Why don't you enjoy beautiful flowers with your loved ones this spring? It will make both of you happy!

Staff reporter Liz Ahn

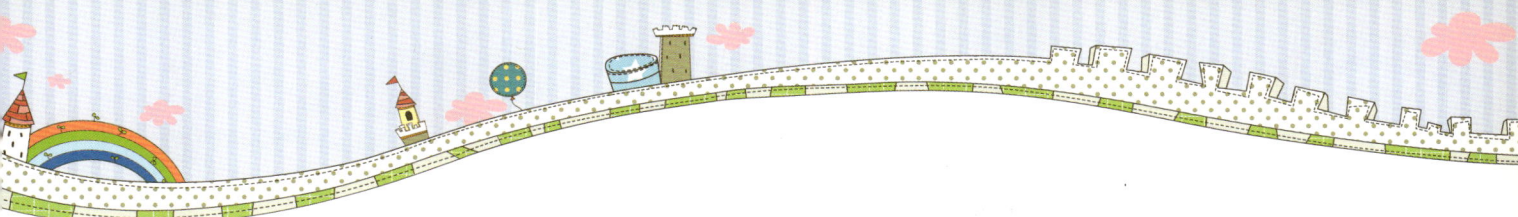

Question 01 — **Writing**

Complete the sentences by filling in the blanks.

(a) All **k** __ __ __ __ of flowers bloom in spring.

(b) The world will be **c** __ __ __ __ __ __ with colorful flowers.

(c) Flowers make our lives more **s** __ __ __ __ __ __.

(d) **G** __ __ __ __ __ flowers to someone is **I** __ __ __ saying "I love you."

(e) Why don't you **e** __ __ __ __ beautiful flowers with your **l** __ __ __ __ ones this spring?

Word Tip

▌kind	▌bloom	▌be covered with	▌colorful
_____	_____	_____	_____
▌special	▌in fact	▌important	▌part
_____	_____	_____	_____
▌loved one	▌for example	▌be used for	▌생일 파티
_____	_____	_____	_____
▌결혼식	▌입학식	▌졸업식	▌어버이날
_____	_____	_____	_____
▌표현하다	▌~하는 것이 어때?		
_____	_____		

Vocabulary I

Let's complete the crossword puzzle.

Words

HAPPY(▶) / EXAMPLE (▶) / FLOWER(▼)

PARENTS (▼) / LOVE (▼) / SPECIAL (▶)

 **Question** ## Vocabulary II

Write down the matching words.

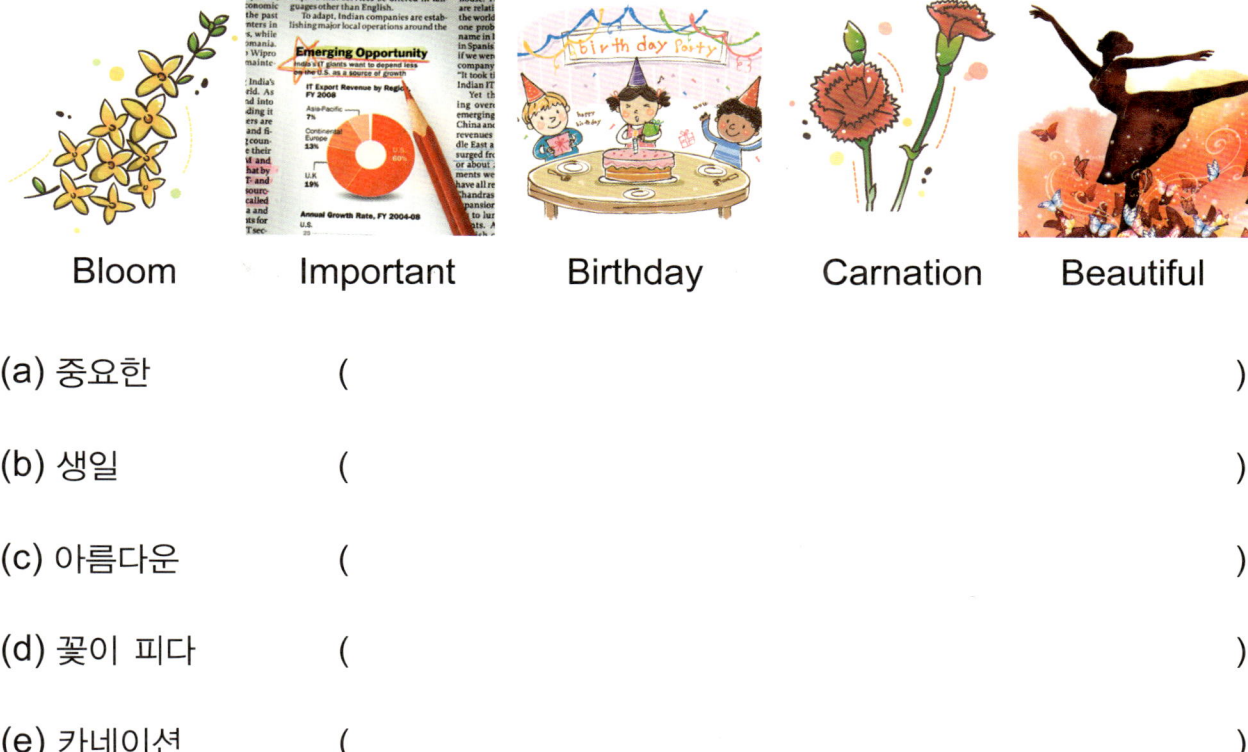

Bloom   Important   Birthday   Carnation   Beautiful

(a) 중요한   (   )

(b) 생일   (   )

(c) 아름다운   (   )

(d) 꽃이 피다   (   )

(e) 카네이션   (   )

 **Question** ## Comprehension

Look at the sentences below. Decide if they are true or false!

(a) Flowers start blooming in winter.   O / X

(b) Flowers are used for birthday parties, entrance ceremonies, and graduation ceremonies.   O / X

(c) Flowers are an important part of our lives.   O / X

(d) We give our parents roses on Parents' Day to express our love.   O / X

Let's Enjoy Chocolate!

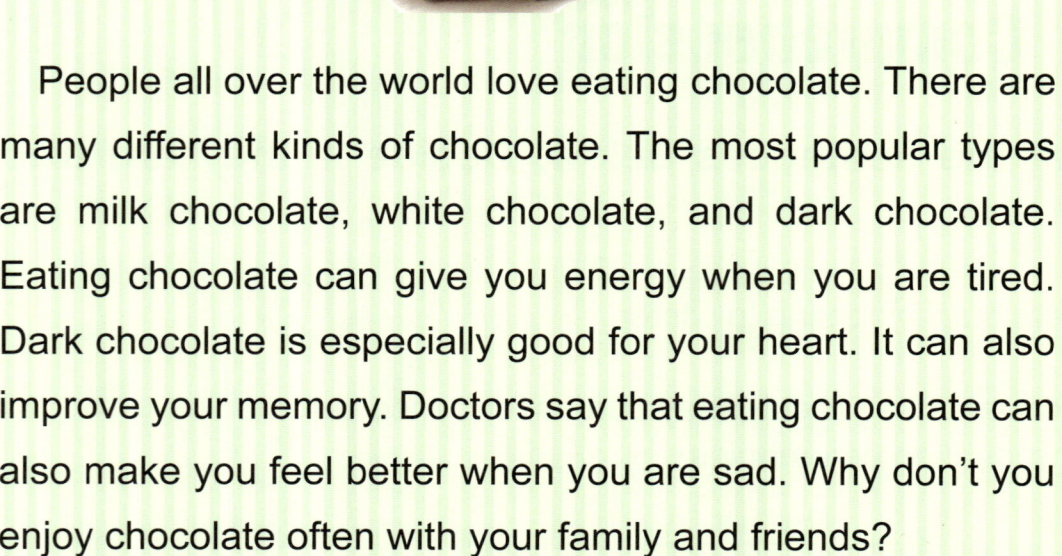

We celebrate Valentine's Day in February. On this day, many people give boxes of chocolates to their loved ones. Chocolate is very delicious. It is good for your health, too!

People all over the world love eating chocolate. There are many different kinds of chocolate. The most popular types are milk chocolate, white chocolate, and dark chocolate. Eating chocolate can give you energy when you are tired. Dark chocolate is especially good for your heart. It can also improve your memory. Doctors say that eating chocolate can also make you feel better when you are sad. Why don't you enjoy chocolate often with your family and friends?

Staff reporter Liz Ahn

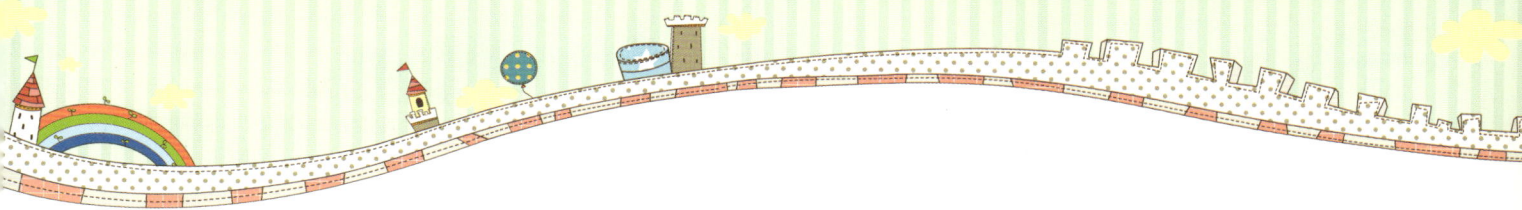

Comprehension

Complete the sentences by filling in the blanks.

(a) Many people _____ boxes of chocolates to their _____ ones on Valentine's Day.

(b) Chocolate is very _____ and good for your _____.

(c) The most _____ _____ are milk chocolate, white chocolate, and dark chocolate.

(d) Eating chocolate can give you _____ when you are _____.

(e) Doctors say that eating chocolate can also make you _____ _____ when you are sad.

Word Tip

▌celebrate	▌Valentine's Day	▌loved	▌delicious
_____	_____	_____	_____
▌be good for	▌health	▌love ~ing	▌kind
_____	_____	_____	_____
▌popular	▌type	▌be tired	▌especially
_____	_____	_____	_____
▌심장	▌개선하다, 향상시키다	▌기억력	▌기분이 나아지다
_____	_____	_____	_____
▌~하는 게 어때요?			
_____			

 **Vocabulary** I

Let's learn how to spell the important words from the article!

(a) **C** __ __ __ __ __ __ __ __

(b) **D** __ __ __ __ __ __ __

(c) **P** __ __ __ __ __ __

(d) **M** __ __ __ __ __

 Question Vocabulary Ⅱ

Find the words below that can be used to describe chocolate.

Failure / Energy / Valentine's Day / Halloween Day
Heart / Stomach / Health / Teach / Memory

(a) **E** __ __ __ __ __

(b) **V** __ __ __ __ __ __ __ __ __
   D __ __

(c) **H** __ __ __ __

(d) **H** __ __ __ __ __

(e) **M** __ __ __ __ __

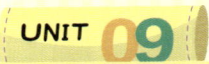

Play Safe at the Playground!

Playing at the playground is always fun. There is so much to do! You can swing. You can play on the seesaw, too. And of course, you can play with many friends! But sometimes kids get hurt at the playground. That's no fun! Let's play safe at the playground.

* Go to the playground with your mom or dad. They can help you if you get hurt.

* If you find something dangerous such as broken glass, don't play there.

* Don't get too close to kids on swings. You can get hurt if you get hit by them.

* Don't push other kids. When there are many kids, you have to wait to swing or slide. Wait for your turn.

* Remember to go home before dark.

Staff reporter Liz Ahn

Read the questions and answer the following.

(a) Look at the words below.

> Push   Lose   Dark   Far   Run   Wait

What are some words that can be used to describe 'play safe' at the playground? Choose three words.

_____, _____, _____

(b) Find the three words that start with "F" in the article.

① **F** __ __ __ __ __

② **F** __ __

③ **F** __ __ __

(c) Which word has the opposite meaning to "Safe"?

D __ __ __ __ __ __ __ __

Word Tip

- playground
  _____
- swing
  _____
- seesaw
  _____
- of course
  _____
- sometimes
  _____
- get hurt
  _____
- safe
  _____
- dangerous
  _____
- broken
  _____
- glass
  _____
- close
  _____
- get hit
  _____
- push
  _____
- have to
  _____
- 기다리다
  _____
- 미끄럼틀
  _____
- 차례, 순서
  _____
- 기억하다
  _____
- 어두워지기 전에
  _____

02 Question **Writing**

Let's make sentences by filling in the blanks, using the words below.

broken / many / play / wait / find

(a) You can _____ on the seesaw.

(b) If you _____ something dangerous such as _____ glass, don't play there.

(c) When there are _____ kids, you have to _____ to swing or slide.

03 Question **Comprehension**

Look at the pictures. Mark "O" for the pictures that show something safe. Mark "X" for the pictures that show something dangerous.

a. (   )

b. (   )

c. (   )

d. (   )

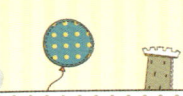

 **Structure**

Match up the pictures and words to make the right sentences.

Sometimes kids get hurt   ⓐ   ① before dark.

Go to the playground   ⓑ   ② at the playground.

Remember to go home   ⓒ   ③ with your mom or dad.

Don't get too close   ⓓ   ④ to kids on swings.

Be a Kind Kid!

Winter is a fun season. You can play in the snow with your friends. You can also go skiing or skating. However, winter is a very difficult season for poor people. Many people don't have warm houses or clothes. Why don't you become a kind kid and help them?

You are still very young, but you can help others, too. Becoming a kind kid is easy. You don't need to have a lot of money or time to help someone. All you need is a warm heart! Just share some of the things you already have. For example, you can give some of your toys, clothes, or books to other children who need them. You can also send pretty cards to the people who need love. There are many other ways to be a kind kid. Think about how to be a kind kid with your friends!

Staff reporter Dan Chun

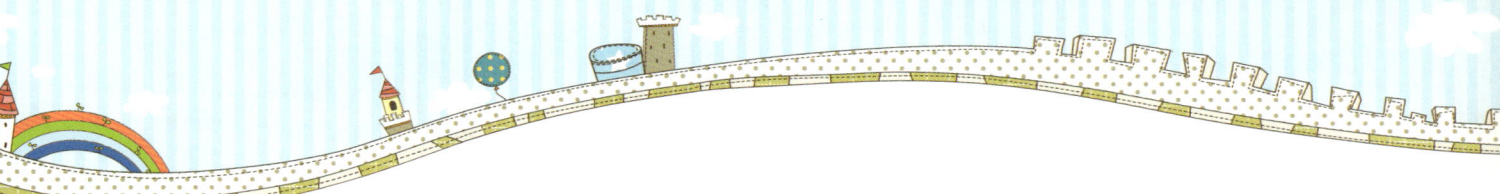

Vocabulary

Read the questions and answer the following.

(a) Look at the words below.

> Love   Mean   Heart   Share   Selfish   Forget

What are some words that can be used to explain how to become a kind kid? Choose three words.

_____, _____, _____

(b) Find the three words that start with "S" in the article.

① **S** __ __ __ __ __

② **S** __ __ __ __ __ __

③ **S** __ __ __ __ __

(c) Which word has the opposite meaning to "Young"?

O __ __

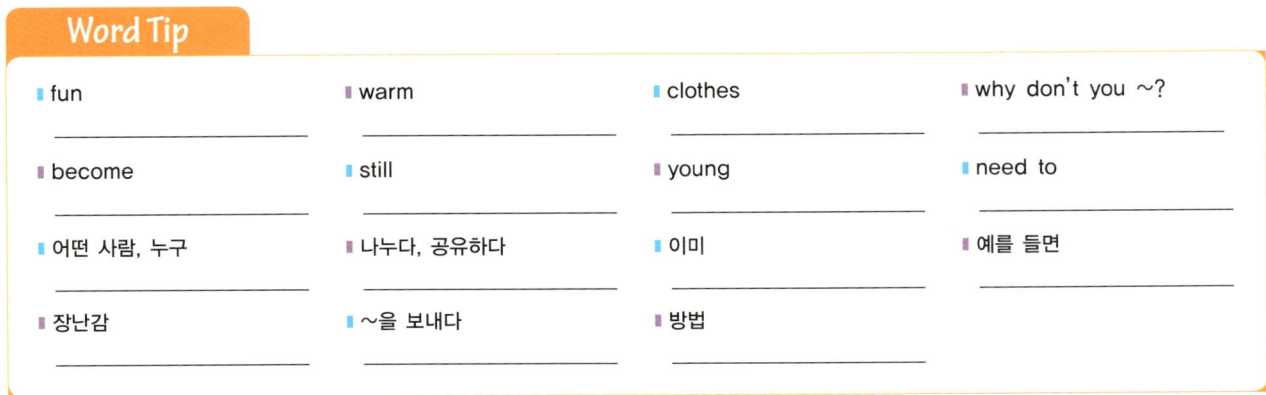

Word Tip			
▌fun	▌warm	▌clothes	▌why don't you ~?
_____	_____	_____	_____
▌become	▌still	▌young	▌need to
_____	_____	_____	_____
▌어떤 사람, 누구	▌나누다, 공유하다	▌이미	▌예를 들면
_____	_____	_____	_____
▌장난감	▌~을 보내다	▌방법	
_____	_____	_____	

Writing

Let's make sentences by filling in the blanks, using the words below.

> become / poor / need / difficult / help / send

(a) Winter is a very __ __ __ __ __ __ __ __ __ season for __ __ __ __ people.

(b) Why don't you __ __ __ __ __ __ a kind kid and __ __ __ __ them?

(c) You can also __ __ __ __ pretty cards to the people who __ __ __ __ love.

Comprehension

Look at the pictures. Mark "O" for the pictures that express being kind. Mark "X" for the pictures that express being mean.

a. ( )

c. ( )

b. ( )

d. ( )

 Question **Structure**

Match up the pictures and words to make the right sentences.

There are many other ways ⓐ

① but you can help others, too.

Just share some of the things ⓑ

② to help someone.

You are still very young ⓒ

③ to be a kind kid.

You don't need to have a lot of money or time ⓓ

④ you already have.

Let's Learn History!

Do you like learning history at school? You may think history is boring. However, learning history is very important. We can learn many things from it. Learning history also helps us better understand the world.

There are many countries in the world. Each country has its own history. Learning other countries' history is important. It helps us better understand them. We are living in a global village. So it is important to understand other countries. A country's past can tell many things about its present and future. Learning our own history is also very important. Our past can teach us many things. Korea has a long history. Many things happened to us in the past. Why don't you start learning Korean history? You will be surprised to learn that Korea is a wonderful country with a long history!

Staff reporter Liz Ahn

Read the questions and answer the following.

(a) Look at the words below.

> Understand   Future   Laugh   Capital   Past

What are some words that tell us how important history is? Choose three words.

_____, _____, _____

(b) Find the four words that start with "L" in the article.

① **L** __ __ __

② **L** __ __ __ __

③ **L** __ __ __ __ __

④ **L** __ __ __

(c) Which word has the opposite meaning to "Start"?

E __ __

Word Tip

▮ learn	▮ history	▮ boring	▮ better
_____	_____	_____	_____
▮ understand	▮ live in	▮ global village	▮ past
_____	_____	_____	_____
▮ 현재	▮ 미래	▮ 가르치다	▮ 일어나다, 발생하다
_____	_____	_____	_____
▮ ~하는 것이 어때?	▮ 놀라다	▮ 훌륭한, 멋진	
_____	_____	_____	

02 Question Writing

Let's make sentences by filling in the blanks, using the words below.

> history / country / boring / surprised / understand

(a) You may think history is _____ .

(b) Learning _____ helps us better _____ the world.

(c) You will be _____ to learn that Korea is a wonderful _____ with a long history!

03 Question Grammar

Circle the right words to complete each sentence.

(a) Do you like [**learn** / **learning** / **learned**] history at school?

(b) A country's past can [**tell** / **told** / **telling**] us many things about its present and future.

(c) Many things [**happens** / **happening** / **happened**] to us in the past.

(d) You may [**think** / **thought** / **thinking**] history is boring.

Structure

Match up the pictures and words to make the right sentences.

We can learn many things ⓐ

① that Korea is a wonderful country with a long history!

Learning history also helps us ⓑ

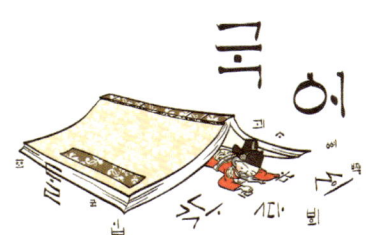

② from history.

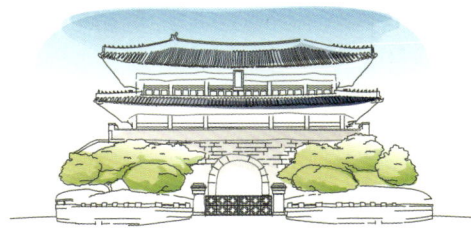

Each country ⓒ

③ better understand the world.

You will be surprised to learn ⓓ

④ has its own history.

Why Is Learning English Important?

Many people in Korea are learning English. Even small children like you learn English, too. Some people enjoy learning it. But some people find it difficult to learn the language. Then, why do we have to learn English? And why is it important to learn it?

We are living in a global village. This means that we have to communicate with foreigners often. But what if they don't speak Korean? Then, you will have to speak in a global language. Today, English is used as a global language in many countries. This is why learning English is important. It helps you communicate with people from other countries easily. It also helps you better understand the world. If you speak English well, you can make many foreign friends, too! When you grow up, you will work with people from all over the world. Speaking English well will help you become a global leader!

Staff reporter Liz Ahn

Complete the sentences by filling in the blanks.

(a) Living in a global village _____ that we have to _____ with foreigners often.

(b) Today, English is _____ as a global _____ in many countries.

(c) English helps you _____ with people from other countries _____.

(d) When you _____ up, you will work with people from all _____ the world.

(e) Speaking English well will help you _____ a global _____!

Word Tip

like	enjoy ~ing	language	then
_____	_____	_____	_____
have to	live in	global village	mean
_____	_____	_____	_____
~와 의사소통 하다	외국인	종종, 자주	~면 어쩌지?
_____	_____	_____	_____
~로 사용되다	중요한	이해하다	성장하다, 자라다
_____	_____	_____	_____
~이 되다			
_____			

02 Question **Vocabulary** I

Let's learn how to spell the important words in the article!

(a) **L** __ __ __ __

(b) **G** __ __ __ __ __

(c) **C** __ __ __ __ __ __ __ __ __ __

(d) **F** __ __ __ __ __ __

 **Vocabulary II**

Find the words below that describe why it is important to learn English.

Weekend / Global / Foreigner / Laugh / Donut
Communicate / Enemy / Friend / Difficult / Understand

(a) **G** __ __ __ __ __

(b) **F** __ __ __ __ __ __ __ __ __

(c) **C** __ __ __ __ __ __ __ __ __ __ __

(d) **F** __ __ __ __ __ __

(e) **U** __ __ __ __ __ __ __ __ __ __

Which Foods Will Bring Good Luck?

We eat rice cake soup on New Year's Day. We believe that eating this delicious food will bring us good luck in the New Year. Which foods are also considered lucky? Read on and find out!

Noodles: People in Japan eat noodles to greet the New Year. They believe that long noodles represent a long life.

Pork: In many countries, pigs are a symbol of good luck. Therefore, many countries all around the world, including Portugal, Austria, Ireland, and Cuba, enjoy pork on New Year's Day.

Green Vegetables: In many countries, bank notes are green in color. People believe that eating green vegetables on New Year's Day will bring wealth in the New Year.

Fish: Fish is eaten in many countries around the world on New Year's Day. People believe that eating fish will bring good luck.

Staff reporter Dan Chun

Complete the sentences by filling in the blanks.

(a) In Korea, we _____ rice cake soup so that it will bring good _____ in the New Year.

(b) People in Japan eat noodles _____ they believe _____ a long life.

(c) In many countries, _____ Portugal, Austria, and Ireland, pigs are a _____ of good luck.

(d) Some people _____ that eating green vegetables will bring _____ in the New Year.

(e) Others _____ the world believe that eating fish will _____ good luck.

Word Tip

▌rice cake soup	▌New Year's Day	▌good luck	▌be considered
_____	_____	_____	_____
▌lucky	▌find out	▌noodle	▌greet
_____	_____	_____	_____
▌나타내다	▌장수	▌돼지고기	▌상징
_____	_____	_____	_____
▌~을 포함하여	▌녹황색 채소	▌지폐	▌가져 오다
_____	_____	_____	_____
▌부, 재산			
_____			

 **Question** **Vocabulary I**

Let's learn how to spell the important words from the article!

(a) **B** __ __ __ __ __ __

(b) **D** __ __ __ __ __ __ __ __

(c) **R** __ __ __ __ __ __ __ __

(d) **W** __ __ __ __ __

03 Question **Vocabulary Ⅱ**

Find the words below that are some of the foods that people eat on New Year's Day.

Cookie / Noodles / Chicken / Curry / Green Vegetables
Pork / Fish / Bananas / Rice Cake Soup / Cereal

(a) **N** __ __ __ __ __ __

(b) **G** __ __ __ __
__ __ __ __ __ __ __ __ __ __

(c) **P** __ __ __

(d) **F** __ __ __

(e) **R** __ __ __ __ __ __ __
__ __ __ __

It's Spring!

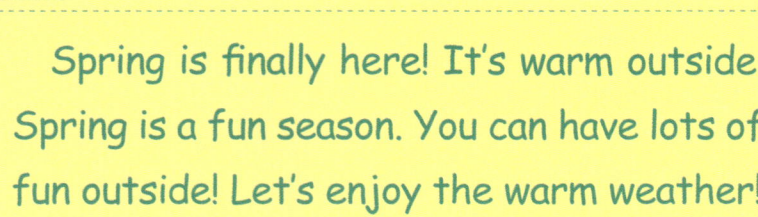

Spring is finally here! It's warm outside. Spring is a fun season. You can have lots of fun outside! Let's enjoy the warm weather!

Family Picnic

Why don't you go on a picnic with your family? Family picnics are always fun! Ask your mom or dad to go to the park on the weekend. Don't forget to bring sandwiches! A picnic without sandwiches is not a picnic!

Playground

Playing with friends is always fun, too! When it's warm outside, go to the playground with your friends. There are swings, slides and seesaws at the playground. When playing with your friends, always be nice to them.

Flowers and Butterflies

Look around! You can see many beautiful flowers. You can also see butterflies. In spring, the world becomes colorful. You can see many different colors. Red, pink, white and yellow flowers and green trees are everywhere!

Staff reporter Liz Ahn

Writing

Complete the sentences by filling in the blanks.

(a) Why don't you go on a **p** __ __ __ __ __ with your family?

(b) When it's warm outside, go to the **p** __ __ __ __ __ __ __ __ __ with your friends.

(c) There are **s** __ __ __ __ __, slides and seesaws at the playground.

(d) In **s** __ __ __ __ __, the world becomes colorful.

(e) Red, pink, white and yellow **f** __ __ __ __ __ __ and green trees are
   e __ __ __ __ __ __ __ __ __!

Word Tip

finally	warm	outside	weather
_____	_____	_____	_____
why don't you ~?	go on a picnic	weekend	forget to
_____	_____	_____	_____
bring	without	playground	swing
_____	_____	_____	_____
미끄럼틀	시소	나비	둘러보다
_____	_____	_____	_____
다채로운, 알록달록한	모든 곳에, 어디나		
_____	_____		

Vocabulary I

Let's complete the crossword puzzle.

Words

TREE (▶) / FAMILY (▼) / SPRING (▶)
PARK (▲) / COLOR (▼) / YELLOW (▶)

03 Question Vocabulary Ⅱ

Write down the matching words.

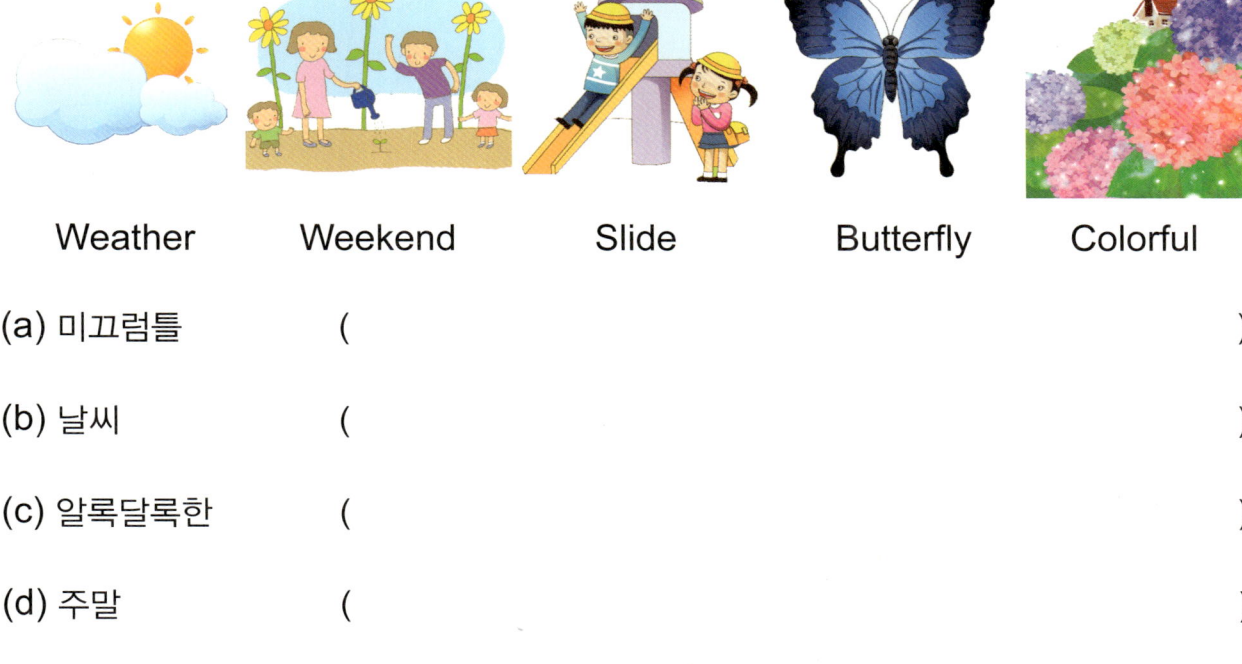

| Weather | Weekend | Slide | Butterfly | Colorful |

(a) 미끄럼틀   (   )

(b) 날씨   (   )

(c) 알록달록한   (   )

(d) 주말   (   )

(e) 나비   (   )

04 Question Comprehension

Look at the sentences below. Decide if they are true or false!

(a) Spring is a warm season.   O / X

(b) You can see colorful flowers in winter.   O / X

(c) Be careful when you play with friends in the playground!   O / X

(d) Bringing sandwiches when going on a picnic with
your family is a bad idea.   O / X

Ask for Help!

Staying safe is very important. No one wants to get hurt. But accidents sometimes happen. Do you know what to do if something dangerous or serious happens? What would you do if your friend or sister got hurt in the playground? Let's learn how to ask for help!

If someone gets hurt, you need to help him or her. Calling for help is the best thing you can do. First, try to stay calm. Then, look around for an adult. Call him or her over to help right away. If no adult is close by, call 119. Tell the operator your name and where you are. Then, explain what happened and how many people are hurt. Also, answer any questions the person asks. Listen carefully to what he or she says. You have to follow everything they say. Go back to the person who got hurt. Stay with him or her until help arrives. Help your friend feel safe and calm.

Staff reporter Dan Chun

Comprehension

Complete the sentences by filling in the blanks.

(a) Staying safe is very _____ but accidents sometimes _____.

(b) Do you _____ what to do if something dangerous or _____ happens?

(c) If someone gets _____, calling for help is the best _____ you can do.

(d) Stay _____ and call 119 if no adult is _____.

(e) _____ everything they say and stay with him or her _____ help arrives.

Word Tip

stay safe	important	accident	happen
_____	_____	_____	_____
serious	ask for	calm	주변을 살펴보다
_____	_____	_____	_____
성인, 어른	즉각, 즉시	가까이에, 인근에	설명하다
_____	_____	_____	_____
사람	도착하다	돌아가다	주의해서 듣다
_____	_____	_____	_____

 **Question** **Vocabulary I**

Let's learn how to spell the important words in the article!

(a) **S** __ __ __

(b) **D** __ __ __ __ __ __ __ __ __

(c) **H** __ __ __

(d) **O** __ __ __ __ __ __ __

Find the words below that are used to express what you should do when someone gets hurt.

Help / Shout / Adult / Fun / Laugh
Sleep / Listen / Follow / Noisy / Calm

(a) **H** __ __ __

(b) **A** __ __ __ __

(c) **L** __ __ __ __ __

(d) **F** __ __ __ __ __

(e) **C** __ __ __

ANSWERS

Word Tip

~에 타격 받다 / 파괴되다, 붕괴되다 / 잃다 / 가족 구성원 / 위험한 / ~해야 한다 / 일어나다, 발생하다 / 노력하다, ~하려고 하다 / 침착하다, 진정하다 / act quickly / get away from ~ / fall on ~ / breakable / item / furniture / look for ~

1. Comprehension
(a) hit, strong
(b) glass, breakable
(c) stay away from
(d) know, happens
(e) Crawl, strong

2. Vocabulary I
(a) Earthquake
(b) Destroy
(c) Fall
(d) Remember

3. Vocabulary II
(a) Cool
(b) Quick
(c) Furniture
(d) Crawl
(e) Hide

UNIT 02

Word Tip

눈을 감다 / 잠시 동안 / 가슴 / 심장 박동 / (심장이) 뛰다, 고동치다 / 항상 / 사실 / blood / throughout / faster / guess / during / lifetime / count

1. Vocabulary
(a) Heart
(b) Home / House / Horse / Hour
(c) It pumps blood throughout my body. So I cannot live without my heart.

2. Writing
(a) chest
(b) beating, organ
(c) count

3. Comprehension
Heart is a very important organ in our body. It pumps blood throughout the body. People cannot live without the heart.

4. Structure
ⓐ – ③
ⓑ – ①
ⓒ – ②

UNIT 03

Word Tip

주위를 둘러보다 / 색채가 풍부한, 화려한 / 계절 / 회색 / 날씨 / 꽃이 피다 / 귀여운 / 나비 / ~로 가득 차다 / 보라색 / 봉오리를 맺다, 눈이 나오다 / 신나는 / 즐기다 / cute / flower / warm / spring / different / winter / in fact

1. Vocabulary
(a) Spring
(b) Spoon / Smile / Sport / Seesaw
(c) I can see many colors in spring. I can see yellow, pink, white, red, orange and green!

2. Writing
(a) colorful
(b) warmer, blooming
(c) filled, with

3. Comprehension
Beautiful purple flowers are blooming. Spring is the most colorful season of the year.
I can see many colorful flowers like pink, yellow and orange flowers in spring. I can see green trees, too!

4. Structure
ⓐ – ②
ⓑ – ③
ⓒ – ①

UNIT 04

Word Tip

계절 / 황사 / 불다 / 포함하다 / 해로운 / 재료 / 일으키다, 야기하다 / 다치다, 다치게 하다 / 목 / 때때로 / 어지러운 / 특히 / try to / stay inside / have to / wear one's mask / wash hands / pork / helpful

1. Vocabulary
(a) Yellow Dust
(b) Young / Yawn / You / Yesterday
(c) Yellow dust can hurt my eyes, nose and throat. It can also make me feel dizzy.

2. Writing
(a) blows over
(b) harmful
(c) inside, closed

3. Comprehension
Yellow dust blows over Korea every year. It is harmful for people's health because it contains many bad things. When yellow dust blows people should stay inside and close windows and doors.

4. Structure
ⓐ – ①
ⓑ – ③
ⓒ – ②

Word Tip

지구 / 동물 / 식물 / 행성 / 놀라운 /
장소 / 배우다 / 재미있는, 흥미로운 /
사실 / 10억 / 돌다 /
~ 주위를 여행하다 / 원, 순환 /
세 번째 / 가장 가까운 / 가장 높은 /
돌출부, 끝 / top / be called /
space / surface /
be covered with ~ / ocean /
Pacific Ocean / largest /
Why don't you ~? / find out

1. Vocabulary

(a) Earth
(b) Ear / Eagle / Eye / Eraser
(c) The Earth is about 4.5
   billion years old.

2. Writing

(a) animals
(b) traveling, around
(c) Planet

3. Comprehension

This is the Earth. The Earth
is home to many animals and
plants. It spins around the Sun
in a big circle. The Earth is also
called the 'Blue Planet'.

4. Structure

ⓐ − ③
ⓑ − ①
ⓒ − ②

Word Tip

옆집(에) / 슬프게도 / 이웃 / 얼굴 /
~으로 바쁘다 / 아마도 / 쓰다, 보내다 /
~와 친구가 되다 / town / of course /
forget to ~ / brightly / remember /
happier

1. Comprehension

(a) know, faces

(b) friends, difficult
(c) help
(d) forget, brightly
(e) Remember, happier

2. Vocabulary I

(a) Door
(b) Busy
(c) Smile
(d) Hello

3. Vocabulary II

(a) Good
(b) First
(c) Help
(d) Smile
(e) Friend

Word Tip

종류 / 꽃이 피다 / ~으로 덮이다 /
색채가 풍부한, 다채로운 / 특별한 /
사실 / 중요한 / 부분 /
사랑하는 사람 / 예를 들어 /
~으로 사용되다 / birthday party /
wedding ceremony /
entrance ceremony /
graduation ceremony /
Parent's Day / express /
Why don't you ~?

1. Writing

(a) kinds
(b) covered
(c) special
(d) Giving, like
(e) enjoy, loved

2. Vocabulary I

3. Vocabulary II

(a) Important
(b) Birthday
(c) Beautiful
(d) Bloom
(e) Carnation

4. Comprehension

(a) X
(b) O
(c) O
(d) X

Word Tip

축하하다, 기념하다 / 발렌타인데이 /
사랑하는 / 맛있는 / ~에 좋다 / 건강 /
~하는 것을 좋아하다 / 종류 /
인기 있는 / 유형 / 피곤하다, 지치다 /
특별히 / heart / improve / memory /
feel better / Why don't you ~?

1. Comprehension

(a) give, loved
(b) delicious, health
(c) popular types
(d) energy, tired
(e) feel better

2. Vocabulary I

(a) Celebrate
(b) Different
(c) Popular
(d) Memory

3. Vocabulary II

(a) Energy
(b) Valentine's Day
(c) Heart
(d) Health
(e) Memory

UNIT 09

Word Tip

놀이터 / 그네 / 시소 / 물론 / 때때로 /
다치다 / 안전한 / 위험한 / 부서진 /
유리 / 가까운 / 얻어맞다, 부딪히다 /
밀다 / ~해야 한다 / wait / slide /
turn / remember / before dark

1. Vocabulary
(a) Push, Dark, Wait
(b) ① Friends
   ② Fun
   ③ Find
(c) Dangerous

2. Writing
(a) play
(b) find, broken
(c) many, wait

3. Comprehension
(a) O
(b) O
(c) X
(d) X

4. Structure
ⓐ – ②, ⓑ – ③
ⓒ – ①, ⓓ – ④

UNIT 10

Word Tip

재미있는 / 따뜻한 / 옷 /
~하는 게 어때요? / ~이 되다 /
아직, 그럼에도 불구하고 / 어린 /
~해야 한다 / someone / share /
already / for example / toy /
send / way

1. Vocabulary
(a) Love, Heart, Share
(b) ① Season
   ② Skating
   ③ Skiing
(c) Old

2. Writing
(a) difficult, poor
(b) become, help
(c) send, need

3. Comprehension
(a) O
(b) O
(c) X
(d) O

4. Structure
ⓐ – ③, ⓑ – ④
ⓒ – ①, ⓓ – ②

UNIT 11

Word Tip

배우다 / 역사 / 지루한 /
더 잘, 더 잘하는 / 이해하다 /
~에 살다 / 지구촌 / 과거 / present /
future / teach / happen /
Why don't you ~? / surprise /
wonderful

1. Vocabulary
(a) Understand, Future, Past
(b) ① Like
   ② Learn
   ③ Living
   ④ Long
(c) End

2. Writing
(a) boring
(b) history, understand
(c) surprised, country

3. Grammar
(a) learning
(b) tell
(c) happened
(d) think

4. Structure
ⓐ – ②, ⓑ – ③
ⓒ – ④, ⓓ – ①

UNIT 12

Word Tip

~와 같은 / ~하는 것을 즐기다 / 언어 /
그러면 / ~해야 한다 / ~에 살다 /
지구촌 / 의미하다 /
communicate with ~ / foreigner /
often / what if ~? / be used as ~ /
important / understand / grow /
become

1. Comprehension
(a) means, communicate
(b) used, language
(c) communicate, easily
(d) grow, over
(e) become, leader

2. Vocabulary I
(a) Learn
(b) Global
(c) Communicate
(d) Friends

3. Vocabulary II
(a) Global
(b) Foreigner
(c) Communicate
(d) Friend
(e) Understand

UNIT 13

Word Tip

떡국 / 새해 / 행운 / ~으로 여겨지다 /
운이 좋은 것, 행운을 가져오는 것 /
찾다 / 국수 / 맞이하다 / represent /
long life / pork / symbol /
including / green vegetable /
bank note / bring / wealth

1. Comprehension
(a) eat, luck
(b) which(or that), represent
(c) including, symbol
(d) believe, wealth

(e) around, bring

2. Vocabulary I
(a) Believe
(b) Delicious
(c) Represent
(d) Wealth

3. Vocabulary II
(a) Noodles
(b) Green Vegetables
(c) Pork
(d) Fish
(e) Rice Cake Soup

4. Comprehension
(a) O
(b) X
(c) O
(d) X

UNIT 15

Word Tip

안전하게 지내다 / 중요한 / 사고 /
일어나다 / 심각한 / 요청하다 /
침착한 / look around / adult /
right away / closed by /
explain / person / arrive /
go back / listen carefully

1. Comprehension
(a) important, happen
(b) know, serious
(c) hurt, thing
(d) calm, close by
(e) Follow, until

2. Vocabulary I
(a) Safe
(b) Dangerous
(c) Hurt
(d) Operator

3. Vocabulary II
(a) Help
(b) Adult
(c) Listen
(d) Follow
(e) Calm

UNIT 14

Word Tip

마침내 / 따뜻한 / 밖 / 날씨 /
~하는 게 어때요? / 소풍 가다 / 주말 /
~을 잊다 / 가져오다 / ~없이 / 놀이터 /
그네 / slide / seesaw / butterfly /
look around / colorful /
everywhere

1. Writing
(a) picnic
(b) playground
(c) swings
(d) spring
(e) flowers, everywhere

2. Vocabulary I

3. Vocabulary II
(a) Slide
(b) Weather
(c) Colorful
(d) Weekend
(e) Butterfly

MEMO